HAL•LEONARD®
VIOLIN
PLAY-ALONG

AUDIO
ACCESS
INCLUDED

Hillsong WORSHIP HITS

T0055876

PLAYBACK+
Speed • Pitch • Balance • Loop

To access audio visit:
www.halleonard.com/mylibrary

Enter Code
2399-6243-6363-3878

ISBN 978-1-5400-3124-2

Jon Vriesacker, violin
Audio arrangements by Peter Deneff
Recorded and Produced by Jake Johnson
at Paradyme Productions

HAL•LEONARD®

Visit Hal Leonard Online at
www.halleonard.com

Contact Us:
Hal Leonard
7777 West Bluemound Road
Milwaukee, WI 53213
Email: info@halleonard.com

In Europe contact:
Hal Leonard Europe Limited
42 Wigmore Street
Marylebone, London, W1U 2RN
Email: info@halleonardeurope.com

In Australia contact:
Hal Leonard Australia Pty. Ltd.
4 Lentara Court
Cheltenham, Victoria, 3192 Australia
Email: info@halleonard.com.au

Broken Vessels
(Amazing Grace)

Words and Music by Joel Houston and Jonas Myrin

Cornerstone

Words and Music by Jonas Myrin, Reuben Morgan, Eric Liljero and Edward Mote

* cue notes optional

Forever Reign

Words and Music by Jason Ingram and Reuben Morgan

Mighty To Save

Words and Music by Ben Fielding and Reuben Morgan

*cue notes optional

rit.

Oceans
(Where Feet May Fail)

Words and Music by Joel Houston, Matt Crocker and Salomon Lighthelm

This I Believe
(The Creed)
Words and Music by Ben Fielding and Matt Crocker

What A Beautiful Name

Words and Music by Ben Fielding and Brooke Ligertwood

O Praise The Name
(Anástasis)

Words and Music by Marty Sampson, Benjamin Hastings and Dean Ussher